New Life, New Land

Women in Early Texas

by

Ann Fears Crawford

Illustrated by Betsy Warren

EAKIN PRESS ★ Austin, Texas

Library of Congress Cataloging-in-Publication Data

Crawford, Ann Fears.
   New life, new land.

   Summary: Presents the experiences of a variety of early women settlers on the
Texas frontier.
   1. Women pioneers — Texas — Juvenile literature. 2. Texas — Social life and
customs — Juvenile literature. 3. Frontier and pioneer life — Texas — Juvenile
literature.
   [1. Women pioneers — texas. 2. Frontier and pioneer life — Texas. 3. Texas —
Social life and customs.]
   I. Warren, Betsy, ill. II. Title.
F391.C79 1986 976.4'0088042 86-16659
ISBN 1-57168-004-7

For

Kathryn Edmundson O'Rourke —
a young woman of today's Texas

About This Book

Many women came to early Texas. They came with their husbands and their children. They came to make a new life in a new land.

Texas seemed strange to these women. Many were not used to life on the frontier. They had to learn new ways of living.

But they helped their husbands make a new life. They helped them farm. They cooked meals and sewed for their families.

Some Texas women worked in the fields. They worked beside their husbands. They hoed cotton. They planted crops. Often they drove the oxen that pulled the plows.

Other women found adventure in Texas. Their lives were often exciting. Some found danger in this new land. All found new homes and new friends.

JANE LONG

One pioneer woman lived a very exciting life in early Texas. Her name was Jane Long. She came to Texas with her husband. He wanted an empire in frontier Texas. He wanted to be a king in a new land.

Often he left Jane on the Texas coast. He went to find soldiers for his army. Jane had only her child and her servant Kian for company.

Once winter came. A storm brought snow and ice.
Jane and Kian cut holes in the ice. They caught fish for
their supper. They shot birds and gathered oysters for
food.

Soon Jane gave birth to a baby girl. Only Kian was
there to help.

One day the Indians came. Jane and Kian were
both afraid.

But they were brave Texas women. Kian quickly loaded the cannon. Jane took off her red petticoat. She ran it up the flagpole. The Indians thought soldiers were at the fort. Then Jane and Kian fired the cannon. The Indians were frightened and ran away.

Then Jane's husband was shot by a Mexican soldier. Jane moved her family to Stephen F. Austin's colony. There she met Sam Houston. Mirabeau B. Lamar wrote a poem for her. He called her "bonnie Jane."

Jane lived a happy life in the republic of Texas. People wrote stories about her adventures. They called her "The Mother of Texas."

MARY RABB

Mary Rabb sat at her spinning wheel. She liked to hear it whistle and whirr. Then she could not hear the Indians. She was so afraid of the Indians she put her pigs under the bed. They were good company, and they made her feel safe.

7

But Mary was often lonely. She and her husband came to Texas with the Rabb family in 1823. But John and Mary had trouble. John could not find good land to farm.

Then Mary's family moved to Texas. John and Mary went to meet them. They packed the horse and oxen. First went their clothes. Then the iron skillet and kettle. Mary's spinning wheel rode on top.

Mary and John set off for the Brazos River. First
came the pigs. Then the cows. Mary and the baby rode
the big horse Tormentor. Last came John jogging along
on the pony Nickety Poly.

How happy Mary's family were to see her!
Everyone sat down to a feast. They ate bear meat, corn
bread, milk, butter, and honey. How good it all tasted!

Then John Rabb was on the move again. He and
Mary camped out on an island. Mary was often afraid.
She was bothered by the mosquitos, flies, and insects.
She was afraid the alligators would eat her children.

One night Mary woke up. She heard water running

near her. The river was on the rise. Mary put out her

hand. The water had risen up to her bed. Mary grabbed

her children and ran for safety.

Mary and her family moved many times. Then John settled down. He found good land and planted corn. Soon he was a rich farmer, and then a businessman. He helped his town grow. Mary Rabb learned to love Texas.

Mary and John had many children. Mary named one of her sons George Washington. But she named another Gail Texas. Mary Rabb was a true pioneer Texas woman.

DILUE ROSE HARRIS

Dilue Rose came to Texas on her birthday. She was eight years old when she first saw her new home.

But Dilue grew to love Texas. She loved the parties and the balls. There Texans danced to "Piney Woods," "Turkey in the Straw," and "Molly Cotton-Tail."

She loved the barbecues, too. There she ate beef, chicken, and deer meat. Everyone enjoyed corn bread, butter, and hot coffee. But Dilue missed cakes. The early settlers had no flour to make them.

Then war broke out. Texans began fighting with Mexico. They wanted to be free from Mexico. General Sam Houston and his men marched to San Jacinto. Santa Anna and his army followed them.

The settlers were afraid. They packed their clothes

and goods, but Dilue also helped the army. She dipped

her spoon in hot lead. She was making bullets for the

Texan army.

Soon the settlers were on the move. They loaded their wagons and oxen. Many walked. Mothers carried their children. The settlers were on the Runaway Scrape. They were leaving Texas. They went toward the Sabine River. They wanted to escape Santa Anna and his army.

Then the rain fell. The creeks and rivers rose. Many people could not get across them. Others became sick. Dilue's beloved baby sister died. Other women and children died, too.

Suddenly the settlers heard horses' hooves. A rider rode up. "Turn back!" he yelled. "Turn back! The danger is over!"

The settlers did not believe him. But Sam Houston's army had beaten the Mexicans. They had won the Battle of San Jacinto. Texas was free.

The weary settlers headed home. They found the Mexicans had burned many houses. Dilue's house still stood. But the Mexicans had torn up the floors. They were looking for hen's eggs.

But the settlers began to build again. They were part of a new republic. It was called the republic of Texas. They had a new government. They even had a president. He was Sam Houston, the hero of the Battle of San Jacinto.

Soon Dilue's father moved his family to Houston. There Dilue went to school. But she still loved parties and balls.

One ball was held each year. It was to honor Sam Houston's victory at San Jacinto. The women wore their best dresses. Some even wore silk dresses. All the men dressed in their best suits.

How Dilue longed to dance with Sam Houston! But
other women were chosen. Then she met Ira Harris.
They fell in love and married. They made their home in
Columbus, Texas.

Dilue lived to see her two sons fight in the Civil War. She often told stories about early days in Texas. She wrote about the Runaway Scrape. To Dilue, "dear old Texas" was always home.

ROSA KLEBERG

Some women came to the republic of Texas from Germany. Rosa Kleberg found life in Texas a great adventure. She found surprises also. There was no white flour in Texas. Rosa had to learn to make corn bread from coarse, yellow flour. How she hated it!

One day an Indian came up to Rosa's kitchen window. He carried two hams. He wanted to swap them for Rosa's fresh baked bread. Rosa was afraid. But she gave the Indian her bread.

Soon she made a friend. She even made clothes for her new Indian friend.

Rosa and her sisters made soap and candles. They washed clothes in an iron pot. They took care of the chickens and milked the cows.

Life in Texas was often hard. Rosa had to sell her best tablecloth to buy rice and flour.

One night Rosa and her husband went to a party. People came in wagons. They wore their best clothes. Everyone danced. All the settlers had a good time. What a surprise Texas was for German Rosa!

MARY AUSTIN HOLLEY

Mary Austin Holley also found surprises in the republic of Texas. How beautiful the land was! She loved the trees, flowers, and birds.

25

Mary played her guitar and wrote stories. She even wrote a song about the Brazos River. She also wrote about Texas for the newspapers. She told about the brave men who fought at the Alamo.

But mostly she wrote about nature. She said Texas was like heaven. Many people read Mary's stories. They read them in newspapers, and they read her book.

Many people came to Texas because of the stories. Mary's stories made Texas seem so beautiful.

MARGARET LEA HOUSTON

Margaret Lea Houston also played her guitar in early Texas. She wrote poems to her husband, too. He was the Texas hero, Sam Houston. But she and her husband were always on the move. How Margaret longed for a home of her own!

Then Sam Houston left for Washington. He was the senator from Texas. First, he built Margaret a house in Texas. Sam and Margaret called it their "Woodland Home."

When Sam was away, Margaret sat by her fireside.
Here she taught her children to read and write. She
told them stories from the Bible.

Margaret also told her children about their father
and how he won the Battle of San Jacinto.

Sam Houston wrote his wife that he was coming home. He wanted to run for governor of Texas. Margaret was happy to have her husband at home at last.

But soon the Houston family was on the move again. Sam Houston was governor of Texas, and the family was moving to Austin. They were going to live in the governor's mansion.

In Austin Margaret Lea had another son. He was the first child born in the governor's mansion. The Houstons named him Temple Lea. Margaret was very happy with her eight children. But she still missed her Woodland Home.

Then the Civil War began. Sam Houston had to make a choice. He believed in the United States. He did not wish to see the United States torn apart.

He did not take the oath to support the South. Sam Houston could no longer serve as governor of Texas.

Margaret and her family moved back to Huntsville. But Sam had sold their Woodland Home. Now the Houstons lived in Steamboat House.

But Margaret had to keep her children quiet! The hero of San Jacinto was dying.

When Sam Houston died, his children were near him. Margaret held his hand. His last words were, "Texas! Margaret! Margaret!"

MARY MAVERICK

One day young Mary Ann Adams went walking
down a country lane in Alabama. She wore her
prettiest green muslin dress.

Young Sam Maverick came riding down the lane
and saw Mary. She was the prettiest girl he had ever
seen. Sam fell in love with Mary right then. He married
her and brought her to Texas.

What a surprise San Antonio was for Mary
Maverick! The houses were made of Mexican adobe.
People bathed in the San Antonio River. Mexican
women washed their clothes nearby.

Sam built Mary a stone house. It had a picket fence around it and fig trees in the yard. Mary planted a garden and began to make butter.

Soon Mary was very happy and busy with her large family of children.

But there was always time for a picnic. Mary loved to bathe in the San Antonio River. She liked to read books, too.

She also loved parties. One day Mary made ice cream and cake. She invited all her friends to a party. Everyone had a good time.

One evening Mary and Sam went to a ball for President Lamar. Mary liked the president of the republic of Texas. He was a poet and very brave. But he did not dance very well.

Life was also filled with danger for Mary and her family. One day the Indians raided San Antonio. They were the Comanches. They were very fierce. Everyone was afraid.

The Indians shot arrows into a room filled with people. Many were killed. The Indians even came into Mary's kitchen. But her servants threw rocks at them. Soon the Indians left.

Sam Maverick was often away from home. Mary missed her husband very much. But he was part of the growing republic of Texas. He served in the Texas government. He also raised cattle.

Many times Sam forgot to brand his calves. They roamed to other ranches. The ranchers rounded them up. They called these calves "mavericks."

Mary was often left at home with her children. Many times they fell ill. Often they were in danger. One day young Agatha's clothes caught fire, but she was saved. The next year she became ill and died.

One day a rattlesnake bit her son George. But he lived to fight in the Civil War. Lewis and Willie also fought for the South.

Mary was proud of all her children. She lived to see her children become citizens of San Antonio. Many were important Texans.

Then Mary wrote about her life in early San Antonio. She wrote about her joys and sorrows. She told about her house and her garden. She wrote about the picnics and the balls. She even told about the Indians.

Afterword

Jane Long. Mary Rabb. Dilue Rose Harris. Rosa Kleberg. Mary Austin Holley. Margaret Lea Houston. Mary Maverick.

These are only a few of the brave women who came to early Texas. They helped build homes and rear families in a new land.

Many women wrote about life in early Texas. They told about their joys and sorrows in early Texas.

Texas women worked hard for their new land. They learned to love their new lives. They were the bright "stars" of the Lone Star State.

WORDS TO KNOW

adventure
frontier
pioneer
empire
oysters
petticoat
colony
mosquitos
mattress
barbecue
settlers
freedom
bullets
republic

government
victory
guitar
poem
governor
mansion
oath
adobe
picket
Comanches
cattle brand
maverick
Civil War
citizens

BOOKS ABOUT TEXAS WOMEN

Author, *Title,* Publisher

Carrington, *Women in Early Texas,* Jenkins
Crawford and Ragsdale, *Women in Texas,* Eakin
Exley, *Texas Tears and Texas Sunshine,* Texas A&M
Lee, *Mary Austin Holley,* University of Texas
Pickrell, *Pioneer Women in Texas,* Pemberton
Ragsdale, *The Golden Free Land,* Landmark
Seale, *Sam Houston's Wife,* University of Oklahoma
Winegarten (ed.), *Texas Women,* Texas Woman's University

ABOUT THE AUTHOR

Ann Fears Crawford has taught for many years in Texas. She has taught junior high, high school, and in college. She has also worked in museums and has been the director of the Sam Houston Memorial Museum. Dr. Crawford has written a number of books about Texas. You will enjoy *¡ Viva ! Famous Mexican Americans, Texas,* and *Women in Texas.*

ABOUT THE ARTIST

Betsy Warren has written many books for young readers. She has also drawn the pictures for many other books. You will enjoy reading her books about Texas. She has written *The Story of Texas, Wildflowers of Texas,* and *Indians Who Lived in Texas.* She has also written *The Thirteen Colonies,* and she has done pictures for *Buffalo and Indians on the Great Plains.*